Fabulous French

Recipes

An Illustrated Cookbook of Sweet Savory Crepe Ideas!

BY: Allie Allen

COOK & ENJOY

Copyright Notes

This book is written as an informational tool. While the author has taken every precaution to ensure the accuracy of the information provided therein, the reader is warned that they assume all risk when following the content. The author will not be held responsible for any damages that may occur as a result of the readers' actions.

The author does not give permission to reproduce this book in any form, including but not limited to: print, social media posts, electronic copies or photocopies, unless permission is expressly given in writing.

Table of Contents

Introduction

How can you bring French crepes into your own kitchen recipe collection?

Will your family enjoy the foray into crepes as much as they like pancakes?

Are the ingredients fairly easy to find, so you can make authentic crepes?

Crepes can certainly be made in your kitchen, by you. And I can almost guarantee that your family will like them at least as well as they like pancakes. The ingredients are easy to find almost anywhere, and the recipes are straightforward and simple to follow.

You can make French crepes either sweet or savory, depending on what meal you're making and what sounds good to you.

Sweet crepes use all-purpose flour, and the batter may be sweetened with vanilla or sugar. They are great for dessert or breakfast. You can serve them with Nutella®, chocolate, fruit, syrup, jams, and jellies. You can even add ice cream.

Savory French crepes are sometimes made using buckwheat flour. They are usually made for lunches or dinners. Some savory fillings include mushrooms and other veggies, eggs, bacon, ham, and cheese. Read on and learn how to make authentic French crepes at home…

French crepes may have originated as a breakfast food. They shine in this role, and they are so tasty, they'll start your day off right.

1 – Golden Egg French Crepes

These crepes have a creamy cheese, ham, and egg filling. It's not a new recipe, but it's still a breakfast favorite.

Makes 8 Servings

Cooking + Prep Time: 55 minutes + 30-60 minutes setting time

Ingredients:

- 3 large eggs, free range if available
- 1 cup of milk, 2%
- 1 cup of beer or soda water
- 1/2 tsp. of salt, kosher
- 3 tbsp. of oil, canola or vegetable
- 1 1/2 cups of flour, all-purpose

For the filling

- 12 separated eggs, large
- 2/3 cup of milk, 2%
- 2 oz. of cheese, parmesan
- 4 slices of ham, chopped finely
- 1/4 cup of melted butter, unsalted
- Salt, kosher, as desired
- Pepper, ground, as desired
- Extra butter, if desired

Instructions:

1. For crepes, combine the flour with kosher salt in medium bowl. Add the eggs, one after another, and beat, creating a batter with a smooth texture.

2. Add the milk, oil, beer or soda water. Continue to beat till smooth. Cover. Allow to set for 30-60 minutes.

3. Heat 6"-7" pan. Dip batter with 1/4 cup measure. Pour in pan and tilt to coat bottom evenly. Turn with spatula. Cook till crepes are thin, and golden brown in color on each side. Stack on plate till you're ready for filling.

4. Preheat the oven to 425F.

5. For filling, beat the milk, egg yolks, cheese, kosher salt ground pepper till fluffy and light. Add melted butter and chopped ham.

6. Whip the 12 egg whites in separate bowl, till they are forming soft peaks. Fold them into yolk mixture.

7. Slowly cook in large pot while continuously stirring. Remove from heat. Add 3 tbsp. butter and stir in. Allow mixture to cool.

8. When finished cooking, stuff the crepes with ham, cheese and egg mixture and roll. Place in buttered baking dish. Refrigerate till time to bake them.

9. Bake the crepes for 8-10 minutes at 425F till bubbly and lightly browned. Serve.

2 – Bacon Egg Breakfast French Crepes

These crepes are not only delicious – they're foolproof, too! The food processor preps the batter and you can use any extra toppings you like.

Makes 7 Servings

Cooking + Prep Time: 45 minutes

Ingredients:

For crepes

- 2 cups of milk, low-fat
- 4 eggs, large
- 3 tbsp. of melted butter, unsalted
- 3/4 tsp. of salt, kosher
- 1 1/2 cups of sifted flour, all-purpose

For the filling

- 8 eggs, large
- 1/4 cup of crumbled bacon
- 1/4 cup of cheese shreds (cheddar, Monterey jack, etc.)

Instructions:

1. Combine crepe ingredients in food processor. Mix till you have a smooth batter.

2. Heat skillet to med-high. Grease with a bit of butter. Whisk 2 tbsp. water with eggs and pour mixture in skillet.

3. Pull outer edge to center as it cooks and scramble eggs. Turn off heat when they're almost done. Season as desired.

4. Spray cooking spray in fry pan on med-low. Pour 1/4 cup of crepe batter in pan. Swirl to cover pan thinly and evenly. Cook for one to two minutes on each side, till browned lightly. Stack crepes as you finish them, till all batter is gone.

5. Cook the cheese and bacon in skillet.

6. Fill the crepes with eggs, bacon and cheese. Roll them up. Add any toppings you like. Serve.

3 – Blueberry Breakfast Crepes

This recipe **Makes** tasty, sweet blueberry filling and topping along with the crepes. You can cut your time by using pre-made crepes.

Makes 4 Servings

Cooking + Prep Time: 45 minutes

Ingredients:

- 1 cup of flour, all-purpose
- 2 eggs, large
- 1/2 cup of milk, low-fat
- 1/2 cup of water, filtered
- 1/4 tsp. of salt, kosher
- 2 tbsp. of unsalted butter, melted

For the filling

- 2 cups of blueberries, fresh
- 1/2 cup of sugar, granulated
- 1 tbsp. of corn starch
- 1 tbsp. of lemon juice, fresh if available
- 1 banana, sliced

Instructions:

1. Whisk eggs and flour together in large bowl. Stir milk and water in slowly. Add butter -and salt. Beat mixture till smooth-textured.

2. Heat a small frying pan on med. Spray lightly with cooking oil. Pour 1/4 cup crepe mixture into pan. This will make one crepe. Swirl pan till batter evenly coats bottom of pan. You want them to be very thin. Cook both sides till golden-brown in color. Remove and set on plate.

3. Place topping ingredients in a pot and constantly stir till it thickens. Add banana slices. Fill crepes and then fold and pour warmed sauce over them. Serve.

4 – Bacon Spinach Breakfast French Crepes

These delicate crepes make an excellent treat for breakfast or brunch. Their savory fillings make them a favorite.

Makes 4 Servings

Cooking + Prep Time: 45 minutes

Ingredients:

- Crepes, prepared
- 6 bacon slices, cooked
- 1 tbsp. of butter, unsalted
- 1/2 lb. of sliced mushrooms, fresh
- 3 tbsp. of butter, unsalted
- 1/4 cup of flour, all-purpose
- 1 cup of milk, low-fat
- 1 x 10-oz. pkg. of frozen thawed, chopped, drained spinach
- 1 tbsp. of chopped parsley, fresh
- 2 tbsp. of Parmesan cheese, grated
- Salt, kosher, as desired
- Pepper, ground, as desired
- 2/3 cup of broth, chicken
- 2 eggs, large
- 1/2 cup of lemon juice, fresh
- Salt, kosher, as desired
- Pepper, ground, as desired

Instructions:

1. Remove crepes from storage dish. Warm them and place wax paper between them.

2. Place the bacon in large skillet. Cook on med-high till browned evenly. Drain the bacon, then crumble it and set it aside.

3. Reserve 1 tbsp. of bacon drippings, then add 1 tbsp. butter and use to sauté the mushrooms.

4. To prepare gravy, melt 3 tbsp. butter on med. heat. Whisk in 1/4 cup of flour while constantly stirring, till it forms a smooth paste. Add one cup of milk while constantly stirring, till it forms a thick, smooth gravy.

5. Add the bacon, spinach, mushrooms, cheese and parsley. Season as desired. Allow to cook till thickened a bit, 8-10 minutes or so. Bring gravy to boil in pan.

6. In small mixing bowl, whisk lemon juice and eggs together. Temper the broth and eggs together while whisking constantly. Season as desired.

7. Fill crepes with meat and spinach filling. Roll them up. Top with warmed egg sauce. Serve.

5 – Jelly Breakfast Crepes

This is a very easy recipe that my family always loves. You can fill them with preserves, jams, or jelly, whatever you prefer.

Makes 2 Servings

Cooking + Prep Time: 20 minutes

Ingredients:

- 1 cup of milk, low-fat
- 1/2 cup of flour, all-purpose
- 3 eggs, large
- A pinch of salt, kosher
- Jam, preserves or jelly, your choice

Instructions:

1. Mix all crepe ingredients together in medium bowl till smooth and blended well.

2. In lightly-greased pan on med-high, dollop batter 1/3 cup per crepe. Swirl pan to spread batter evenly.

3. Cook till bottom of crepe is browned lightly. Flip. Cook other side. Remove crepe from the pan.

4. Repeat with remaining batter.

5. Fill with jam, jelly, etc. Serve.

6 – Ham, Cheese Egg Breakfast French Crepes

These crepes have a delicious filling and they pack plenty of protein, so they will keep you from getting hungry till lunch. You can easily freeze and thaw leftovers, too.

Makes 10 Servings

Cooking + Prep Time: 25 minutes

Ingredients:

- Prepared crepes

For filling

- 1 to 2 tbsp. of mustard, Dijon
- 1/3 pound of strip-cut deli ham
- 10 eggs, large – scramble with 4 tbsp. of milk or heavy cream
- 8 ounces of shredded cheddar cheese

Instructions:

1. Melt 1/2 tbsp. of butter in non-stick pan. Sauté scrambled eggs. Cook till fluffy and somewhat moist. Set the eggs aside and allow to cool.

2. Lightly brush one side of first crepe with mustard. Place pinch of cheese in middle. Top with eggs, ham, then more shredded cheese. Roll crepe to close. Repeat this step with remainder of crepes.

3. Sauté in unsalted butter for three minutes on each side on med-low heat till both sides are golden brown. Serve.

7 – French Crepes Benedict

This is an amazing and simple twist on a classic breakfast favorite. Next time you're hungry for eggs benedict, try French crepes benedict.

Makes 8 Servings

Cooking + Prep Time: 20 minutes

Ingredients:

- 12 large eggs, free-range if available
- Salt, kosher, as desired
- Pepper, ground, as desired
- 2 tbsp. of butter, unsalted
- 8 heated ham slices, thin
- 8 crepes, pre-made
- Hollandaise Sauce, bottled

Instructions:

1. Beat the eggs. Season as desired.

2. Melt the butter. Scramble the eggs softly in pan with butter.

3. Place crepes out and warm them before assembling.

4. Place a slice of ham on every crepe. Spoon the eggs atop ham. Fold the crepe and its ham over the eggs. Top with warmed Hollandaise sauce and serve.

8 – Spinach Ham Breakfast Crepes

The French crepes in this recipe hold delicious spinach, ham, and cheese. It's a time-saver, too, since you're using prepared French crepes.

Makes 4 Servings

Cooking + Prep Time: 1/2 hour

Ingredients:

- 8 crepes, prepared
- 1/2 sliced onion, yellow or white
- 2 minced garlic cloves
- 1 cup of spinach, fresh
- 4 slices of cheese, Swiss or mozzarella
- 8 ham slices
- 4 eggs, fried

Instructions:

1. Heat non-stick pan on med. heat.

2. Add butter and sliced onions to pan. Cook till browned well.

3. Add the spinach, garlic and kosher salt. Stir till spinach wilts.

4. Remove spinach mixture.

5. Lay prepared crepes on baking sheet.

6. Place a cheese slice in center of each crepe.

7. Top cheese slice with a couple ham slices and some spinach mixture.

8. Top with fried egg. Fold crepe edges over egg and press down. Repeat with remainder of crepe.

9. Bake crepes for five minutes, till yolk is at the consistency you prefer. Serve.

9 – Raisin Apple Crepes

This tasty recipe uses applesauce instead of pureed apples, to save time. You can put any filling you like in these crepes.

Makes 4 Servings

Cooking + Prep Time: 35 minutes

Ingredients:

- 1 cup of flour, all-purpose
- 2 eggs, large
- 1/2 cup of milk, low-fat
- 1/2 cup of water, filtered
- 1/4 tsp. of salt, kosher
- 2 tbsp. of unsalted butter, melted

For topping: maple syrup, as desired

For the filling

- 1/2 cup of applesauce
- 1/4 cup of raisins, regular or golden
- 2 tbsp. of sugar, brown
- 1/4 tsp. of cinnamon, ground

Instructions:

1. Whisk eggs and flour together in large bowl. Stir in water and milk slowly. Add butter and kosher salt. Beat mixture till smooth.

2. Heat small frying pan on med. heat. Spray lightly with cooking oil.

3. Pour crepe batter into pan, about 1/4 cup batter per crepe. Swirl pan and coat bottom.

4. Cook on both sides till golden brown. Remove and place on plate.

5. Mix applesauce, brown sugar, cinnamon and raisins together well. Heat mixture in the microwave for two minutes or so. Spoon about 2 tbsp. in each crepe. Fold. Serve with maple syrup or extra applesauce mixture on top.

10 – Vanilla Breakfast Crepes

In our family, vanilla crepes are a Sunday morning treat. The smell of vanilla as they cook is so inviting, everyone wants some.

Makes 6 Servings

Cooking + Prep Time: 35 minutes

Ingredients:

- 1 1/2 cups of milk, low-fat
- 3 yolks from large eggs
- 2 tbsp. of vanilla extract, pure
- 1 1/2 cups of flour, all-purpose
- 2 tbsp. of sugar, granulated
- 1/2 tsp. of salt, kosher
- 5 tbsp. of unsalted butter, melted

Instructions:

1. In large mixing bowl, combine milk, vanilla and egg yolks. Stir in flour, salt, sugar and the melted butter till blended well.

2. Heat pan on med. heat till hot. Then coat with oil. Pour 1/4 cup of the batter in middle of pan. Swirl pan so entire bottom is covered. When you see bubbles forming and edges have dried a bit, flip crepe and cook till lightly browned. Repeat with the rest of the batter.

3. Fill the vanilla crepes with some of your favorites: cheese, caramel, fruit, etc. Serve.

Savory lunch and dinner French crepes are popular, too. Try one soon!

11 – Savory Tomato Cheese Crepes

These crepes are filled with tomato and cheese. This recipe features buckwheat crepes, and they have a unique and enticing taste.

Makes 4 Servings

Cooking + Prep Time: 50 minutes + 8 hours refrigeration time

Ingredients:

- 1 1/2 cups of milk, low-fat
- 2 eggs, large
- 2 tbsp. of butter, unsalted
- 3/4 cup of flour, all-purpose
- 1/4 cup of flour, buckwheat
- 1 pinch of salt, kosher
- 3 tbsp. of butter, unsalted
- 1/2 cup of sliced mushrooms, cremini if available
- 1 cup of tomatoes, diced
- 2 cups of spinach leaves, baby
- 4 tsp. of butter, unsalted
- 1 cup of Gruyere cheese shreds

Instructions:

1. Combine the milk, 2 tbsp. of butter and the eggs in food processor. Add both flours and 1 pinch salt. Puree till smooth. Place the batter in refrigerator and allow to rest overnight.

2. Melt 3 tbsp. unsalted butter in large sized skillet on med-high. Stir in the cremini mushrooms. Cook till golden brown in color, 8-10 minutes. Add the spinach and tomatoes. Stir while cooking till spinach wilts, three to four minutes. Set filling aside.

3. Melt a tsp. of unsalted butter in large-sized skillet on med. meat. Then pour in about 1/4 cup of batter in skillet. Swirl pan to fill bottom evenly and thinly. Cook till center sets and edges start browning, three to four minutes.

4. Repeat step 3 with remainder of batter.

5. Sprinkle 1/4 filling in middle of crepes. Sprinkle with 3 tbsp. each of Gruyere cheese shreds. Reserve the rest of the cheese.

6. Fold crepes into thirds around filling, which forms triangles. Serve the crepes with the rest of the cheese sprinkled over the tops.

12 – Seafood Crepe

These French crepes are wrapped around this delectable mixture of crab meat and shrimp. They are as delicious as they are elegant.

Makes 8 Servings

Cooking + Prep Time: 1 hour 5 minutes

Ingredients:

- 8 crepes, pre-made

For filling

- 1 tbsp. of butter, unsalted
- 1 chopped garlic clove
- 1 x 8-ounce package of cubed cream cheese, light
- 1 pound of frozen, thawed medium shrimp, cooked
- 1 x 6-ounce can of flaked, drained crab meat
- 1/2 cup of tomato sauce, low sodium
- 1 tsp. of nutmeg, ground

Instructions:

1. Melt 1 tbsp. of butter in small pan over med. heat. Add the garlic. Stir while cooking for two minutes. Add cream cheese gradually and stir till melted completely.

2. Add the crab meat, shrimp tomato sauce and stir well. Cook for 8-10 minutes, till heated fully through.

3. Spoon 1/8 seafood mixture over middle of crepes and roll them up. Lightly sprinkle using the ground nutmeg and serve.

13 – Chicken Curry Olive Crepes

This is one of my family's favorite French crepe recipes. It's a flavorful dish that is well-suited as a meal served to guests.

Makes 6-8 Servings

Cooking + Prep Time: 50 minutes

Ingredients:

For the crepes:

- 2 1/2 cups of milk, 2%
- 1 1/2 cups of flour, all-purpose
- 3 beaten eggs, medium
- 2 tbsp. of oil, vegetable
- 1/2 tsp. of salt, kosher

For the filling:

- 1/4 cup of butter, unsalted
- 1 cup of onion, diced
- 1 1/4 cups of celery, diced
- 2 tbsp. of flour, all-purpose
- 1 tsp. of salt, kosher
- 1 cup of milk, 2%
- 3/4 tsp. of curry powder
- 2 bouillon cubes, chicken
- 1/2 cup of filtered water, warm
- 3/4 cup of sliced olives, black
- 2 1/2 cups of chicken meat, breast, diced and cooked
- 1/4 cup of Parmesan cheese, grated

Instructions:

1. In medium mixing bowl, combine milk, oil, eggs, flour and kosher salt. Beat together well for a minute till your batter is thin and smooth.

2. Grease a skillet lightly. Place on med. heat. Pour in thin layer of the crepe batter and swirl till it covers the bottom of your pan. Brown on just one side. Repeat till you have used all batter. Set aside.

3. Melt the butter in skillet on med. heat Sauté onions and celery till barely tender. Then stir in the curry, flour and salt and blend well.

4. Dissolve the chicken bouillon in filtered water. Pour this mixture together with milk in skillet and stir till thickened and mixed well. Add chicken and olives. Mix all ingredients together well.

5. Preheat the oven to 400F.

6. Scoop some filling mixture on middle of crepes. Leave enough room to easily fold them like burritos. Fold crepes. Lightly grease a 13" x 9" casserole dish. Place folded crepes in dish. Sprinkle the tops with cheese.

7. Bake in 400F oven to 10-12 minutes, till cheese has melted. Serve.

14 – Chicken Garlic Crepes

These crepes are easy to make ahead of time. Then, for brunch or dinner, you can just add your favorite types of fillings for a satisfying and delicious meal.

Makes 15 Servings

Cooking + Prep Time: 1 hour 10 minutes

Ingredients:

- Crepes, prepared

For the filling

- 5 tbsp. of butter, unsalted
- 4 minced garlic cloves
- 2 tsp. of chopped thyme, fresh
- 2 1/2 cups of rotisserie chicken, shredded
- 1/3 cup of light cream cheese, garlic herb
- 2 tbsp. of chopped parsley, fresh

Instructions:

1. Warm the crepes.

2. To prepare the filling, melt 3 tbsp. butter in skillet on med-high. Add thyme and garlic. Add the chicken. Stir while cooking for five minutes, till heated fully through. Add and stir in the cream cheese till smooth and melted.

3. Remove skillet from heat. Divide chicken and garlic mixture in middle of crepes. Roll them up. Place them in a shallow baking dish and overlap them a bit. Melt the last 2 tbsp. of butter. Drizzle it over the crepes.

4. Place baking dish in oven at 350F and cook for 8-10 minutes, till warmed fully through. Sprinkle with the parsley and serve.

15 – Southwestern Sausage Bell Pepper Crepes

Making crepes need not be an intimidating thing. They're actually easy to make and you can fill them with many different savory tastes, like this sausage and bell pepper mixture.

Makes 7 Servings

Cooking + Prep Time: 55 minutes

Ingredients:

For the filling

- 1 lb. of pork sausage, ground
- 1 diced onion, small
- 1 seeded, diced bell pepper, red
- 2 cups of sliced mushrooms, fresh
- 1/4 cup of chopped cilantro
- 5 eggs, large
- 6 whites from large eggs
- 1/4 cup of milk, 2%
- 1 cup of cheddar cheese shreds
- Salt, kosher, as desired
- Pepper, ground, as desired
- 6 yolks from large eggs
- 3/4 cup of butter, unsalted
- 2 juiced lemons, fresh

For crepes

- 1 cup of flour, all-purpose
- 1 egg, large
- 2 cups of milk, 2%
- 1 x 16-oz. jar of salsa, mild or medium

To garnish: a pinch of paprika

Instructions:

1. Cook the sausage on med. heat in large sized skillet. When it has cooked halfway through, drain away most fat.

2. Add cilantro, mushrooms, red peppers and onions. Cook till veggies become tender and sausage has fully browned. Then remove them from pan, leaving just a light oil coating.

3. Whisk five eggs with 1/4 cup milk cheese and egg whites. Return the skillet to med-high heat. Add egg mixture. Stir occasionally while cooking till eggs have set. Remove from the heat. Keep warm.

4. In large pot on med. heat, combine the lemon juice, egg yolks and butter. Whisk the mixture continuously, while watching heat level so mixture won't curdle. Remove skillet from the burner when the butter is fully melted.

5. In medium sized bowl, whisk milk, flour and egg together. Pour through fine sieve, eliminating lumps.

6. Heat small pan over med-high. Spray with non-stick spray, then pour 1/3 cup of crepe batter into pan. Swirl pan to cover bottom thinly. Flip crepe when bubbling starts. Cook till both sides are lightly golden. Repeat till you use all the batter.

7. Place crepes on medium plates. Spoon sausage and egg mixture down center of crepes. Fold over into half-circles. Sprinkle with a bit of paprika. Serve with salsa.

16 – Mushroom, Cheese Spinach Crepes

These crepes offer a unique combination of tastes that work well together. My family always asks for these at least once a week.

Makes 4 Servings

Cooking + Prep Time: 55 minutes

Ingredients:

- 12 x 6" crepes, premade
- 3 tbsp. of oil, olive
- 1 1/4 pounds of trimmed, thin-sliced, rinsed mushrooms
- 1/4 cup of fine-chopped parsley, flat-leaf
- 1 tbsp. of thyme leaves, fresh
- 1 chopped clove of garlic
- Salt, kosher, as desired
- Pepper, ground, as desired
- 1 x 10-oz. pkg. of washed, de-stemmed, chopped spinach, fresh
- 5 oz. of crumbled goat cheese
- 2 cups of shredded mozzarella cheese

Instructions:

1. Warm the crepes and set them aside.

2. Preheat the oven to 350F.

3. Heat oil in large-sized skillet till a slice of mushroom sizzles. Add mushrooms in one batch. Stir while cooking on med-high till they start browning, 8-10 minutes.

4. Add and stir in garlic, thyme and parsley. Season as desired and cook for a minute.

5. Reduce the heat level to med. Stir in spinach. Cover. Cook till spinach barely wilts, one to two minutes.

6. Remove cover. Add goat cheese and stir till it melts.

7. Spoon the mixture down middle of crepes and roll them up. Arrange them in a line in 13" x 9" casserole dish and sprinkle them with shredded mozzarella.

8. Cover dish with aluminum foil. Heat till the cheese melts, 12-15 minutes or so. Serve crepes warm.

17 – Turkey Tarragon Crepes

This recipe is a great way to use up leftover turkey. You can use different spices, if tarragon isn't a favorite, and the flavor will still astound you.

Makes 12 Servings

Cooking + Prep Time: 45 minutes

Ingredients:

- 12 crepes, pre-made

For filling

- 4 tbsp. of butter, unsalted
- 2 tbsp. of onion, chopped finely
- 4 tbsp. of flour, all-purpose
- 1 cup + 1/4 cup of milk, low-fat
- 3/4 cup of chicken broth, low sodium
- 1/4 cup of white wine, dry
- 1/4 tsp. of chopped tarragon, dried
- 2 yolks from large eggs
- 2 cups of diced chicken, cooked
- A pinch of salt, kosher, +/- as desired

Instructions:

1. Preheat the oven to 350F. Warm the crepes.

2. Melt the butter in pan on med. heat. Add and stir onions. Cook for two minutes. Stir flour in and blend well.

3. Whisk in one cup of milk slowly and whisk constantly till smooth. Add and mix in the wine, broth and dried tarragon. Stir on med-low till it thickens, three to four minutes.

4. In small mixing bowl, stir 3 tbsp, broth and hot milk sauce gradually into egg yolks.

5. Pour the egg mixture into your sauce and briskly whisk. Cook for one more minute, and then remove pan from the heat.

6. Mix 1/2 sauce with chicken in medium mixing bowl. Season as desired.

7. Fill warmed crepes with 3 tbsp. each of the chicken mixture and roll them up. Place with seam side facing down in 13" x 9" casserole dish. Use 1/4 cup of milk to thin remainder of sauce. Pour it over top of crepes.

8. Bake in 350F oven for 18-20 minutes, till sauce starts bubbling. Serve.

18 – Tomato Basil Crepes

The oat crepes in this recipe are handily stuffed with tomatoes, perky basil, and soft cheese. They make a perfect summer dinner when you want to eat light.

Makes 8-10 Servings

Cooking + Prep Time: 10 minutes

Ingredients:

- 2 oat crepes, pre-made

Filling (enough for two crepes)

- 1 oz. of cheese, goat
- 5 or 6 thin tomato slices
- 1 tbsp. of minced basil

Instructions:

1. Warm pre-made crepes in skillet on med. heat with a bit of oil.

2. Spread goat cheese on the crepes. Layer the tomatoes over the cheese. Sprinkle with the basil. Fold the crepes in half. Place in skillet.

3. Cook crepes on both sides till they are browning, and filling has heated through. Serve.

19 – Mushroom Cheese Crepes

These delicious crepes will be filled with mushrooms, cheese, and scrambled egg whites. The dish **Makes** an impressive dinner for guests.

Makes 8 Servings

Cooking + Prep Time: 50 minutes

Ingredients:

- 5 tbsp. of butter, unsalted
- 3 large eggs, whole
- 1 cup of milk, 2%
- 3/4 cup of flour, all-purpose
- 5 tbsp. of sugar, granulated
- 1/4 tsp. of salt, kosher
- 2 cups of sliced mushrooms, fresh
- 16 lightly beaten whites from large eggs
- 1 x 8-oz. pkg. of three cheese blend, shredded
- 3 thin-sliced onions, green

Instructions:

1. Heat the oven to 350F.

2. Melt 3 tbsp. of butter and add to milk and whole eggs in large mixing bowl. Whisk till blended well. Add the flour, salt and 2 tbsp. of sugar. Mix thoroughly.

3. Spray a small skillet with non-stick spray. Heat over med-high. Add 1/4 cup of batter and swirl skillet so batter covers bottom evenly and thinly. Cook for one to two minutes, till bottom has browned lightly, then cook for 20 seconds more. Transfer the crepe to a warmed plate.

4. Repeat these steps with the rest of the batter, making eight crepes.

5. Stir while cooking the mushrooms in large sized skillet in 1 tbsp. of remaining butter, for three to five minutes, or till they are tender. Add the remainder of butter, then the egg whites. Cook for three to five minutes, occasionally stirring, till eggs have set.

6. Top the crepes using onions, scrambled eggs, mushrooms and cheese and fold them in half. Place in a 13" x 9" in casserole dish.

7. Bake in 350F oven till cheese melts. Serve.

Dessert crepes are so tasty and sweet, they're hard to resist. Here are some of the best...

20 – Apricot Crepes

The filling in this recipe is made with a bit of brandy and apricot jam, making the crepes delicious and elegant. Pre-made crepes work well here.

Makes 4 Servings

Cooking + Prep Time: 15 minutes

Ingredients:

- Crepes, pre-made

For the filling

- 1/2 cup of jam, apricot
- 2 tbsp. of butter, unsalted
- 2 tbsp. of brandy

Optional: almond slivers, toasted

Instructions:

1. Set crepes on plate and warm in microwave before filling.

2. In small pan on med. heat, combine brandy, jam and butter.

3. Occasionally stir till blended well. Reduce the heat level to low. Continue stirring occasionally.

4. Brush crepes with heaping tsp. of filling. Fold or roll crepes. Drizzle extra filling over crepes. Sprinkle with powdered sugar and toasted almonds as desired. Serve.

21 – Blackberry Lemonade Cream Cheese Dessert Crepes

Crepes are a delicious dessert, to be sure. These blackberry, lemonade, and cream cheese crepes are wonderfully original. The flavors accent each other so well.

Makes 8 Servings

Cooking + Prep Time: 1 1/4 hour

Ingredients:

For the crepes

- 2 eggs, medium
- 2 tbsp. sugar, granulated
- 1 tsp. of vanilla, pure
- 1/4 tsp. of cinnamon, ground
- 1/8 tsp of salt, kosher
- 2 cups milk, low-fat
- 1 cup flour, all-purpose
- 1 tbsp. of melted butter, unsalted

For Lemonade Cream Cheese Filling

- 2 x 8-ounce pkgs. of cream cheese, reduced fat
- 1 box of lemon pudding/pie filling, instant
- 3/4 cup of concentrate, lemonade
- 1 x 5-ounce can of milk, evaporated

For the Blackberry Filling

- 4 cups of blackberries, fresh
- 1/2 cup of sugar, granulated
- 3 tbsp. of lemon juice, fresh if available
- 7 tbsp. of water, filtered
- 3 tsp. of corn starch

Instructions:

1. To prepare crepes, whisk eggs in mixing bowl. Add remainder of ingredients. Beat at med. speed till blended well. Heat small pan on med. heat. Add a bit of butter.

2. Add 1/2 cup of crepe mixture to the pan. Swirl and cover pan bottom.

3. Cook for one to two minutes, till edges of crepe begin browning. Flip and cook for about a minute more. Repeat with all crepes.

4. To prepare lemonade and cream cheese filling, beat the cream cheese in mixing bowl for three minutes.

5. Add the lemonade concentrate. Beat for one minute more and set bowl aside.

6. In medium-sized bowl, add the evaporated milk and lemon flavored pudding mix. Beat for two minutes. It should be quite thick.

7. Add the pudding mixture to the cream cheese and lemonade mixture. Beat for one minute. Place in refrigerator till you're prepared to serve.

8. To prepare the blackberry filling, add 4 tbsp. of water, lemon juice, sugar and blackberries to medium pan. Bring to boil.

9. In small-sized bowl, mix three tbsp. water with the corn starch. Pour this mixture into the blackberries. Continue to cook till thickened, while smashing blackberries a little. Remove from the heat when blackberries have cooked as you desire. Allow them to cool.

10. Take one crepe. Spread thin layer of the lemonade filling, followed by blackberry filling on the whole crepe.

11. Roll each of the crepes. Sprinkle with confectioner's sugar. Serve.

22 – Rum Pineapple Crepes

This recipe isn't a quick one to fix, but it will truly impress any guests you have over for a meal and dessert. The pineapple and rum mixture is delicious and sophisticated.

Makes 6 Servings

Cooking + Prep Time: 55 minutes + 2-3 hours refrigeration time

Ingredients:

- 4 eggs, large
- 1 1/2 cups of milk, low-fat
- 1 1/2 cups of flour, all-purpose
- 1/8 tsp. of salt, kosher
- 1 tsp. of sugar, granulated
- 2 tsp. of melted butter, unsalted

For Sauce

- 2 tsp. of butter, unsalted
- 1 tsp. of sugar, brown
- 1 tsp. of sugar, granulated
- 3 oz. of rum, dark
- 2 cups of diced pineapple, fresh
- 1/3 tsp. of cinnamon, ground
- 1/2 cup of juice, pineapple
- 1 cup of whipped cream, lightly sweetened
- 1/4 cup of toasted almonds, sliced
- 1/3 cup raisins

To garnish: powdered sugar and mint sprigs

Instructions:

1. Prepare the batter for crepes by whisking together the milk and eggs. Sift the flour, sugar and kosher salt into separate bowl.

2. Incorporate dry mixture into wet mixture. Mix very well and break up lumps, if any. Whisk till the batter has a smooth consistency. Add the melted butter. Mix again. Place batter in refrigerator for two to three hours or longer.

3. To prepare crepes, heat non-stick pan on med. heat. Pour in two to three tbsp. batter. Swirl so bottom of pan is evenly coated. Cook for about a minute, till batter has set. Flip the crepe and cook till a light golden brown in color. Slide crepe from the pan. Repeat till you have used all batter. Keep cooked crepes warm.

4. Melt the butter in medium pan. Add the pineapple, sugars, cinnamon and raisins and sauté them briefly. Then remove the pan from heat. Add the rum.

5. Carefully return pan to stove top burner, since rum can flame up. Simmer for a minute. Add the pineapple juice. Simmer till sauce has slightly thickened.

6. Fold crepes. Place them on individual plates. Top with the rum and pineapple mixture. Use whipped cream and almonds to garnish. Dust with powdered sugar. Add sprigs of mint and serve.

23 – Banana Strawberry Crepes

We have guests over for brunch sometimes, and they love these fruit-topped crepes. To save time, you can make the crepes on the previous night and keep them in the fridge to fill the next day.

Makes 9 Servings

Cooking + Prep Time: 35 minutes + chilling time

Ingredients:

- 1 cup of flour, all-purpose
- 1 tbsp. of sugar, granulated
- 1/2 tsp. of cinnamon, ground
- 1 1/2 cups of milk, low-fat
- 2 eggs, large
- 1-2 tbsp. of butter, unsalted

For the filling

- 1 x 8-oz. pkg. of softened cream cheese, light
- 1 x 8-oz. carton of frozen, thawed whipped topping
- 1/2 cup of sugar, powdered

For the topping

- 1 cups of sliced strawberries, fresh
- 2 sliced medium bananas, firm

Optional: 1 cup of sugar, granulated

Instructions:

1. In large mixing bowl, combine milk, eggs, cinnamon, sugar and flour. Cover. Place in refrigerator for an hour.

2. In small skillet, melt 1 tsp. of butter. Star the batter and drop 2 tbsp. in middle of skillet. Swirl and coat bottom evenly. Cook till the top looks dry, then flip and cook for 15 to 20 longer seconds. Remove to wire rack.

3. Repeat step 2 with remainder of batter. Add more butter to skillet if you need it. Stack crepes and keep warm till you need them.

4. In large-sized bowl, beat filling ingredients till you have a smooth texture. Spread two tbsp. on each individual crepe. Roll the crepes up. Combine the toppings and spoon over the crepes. Serve.

24 – Danish Cream Cheese Dessert Crepes

This dessert features Danish taste in French crepes. They are delicious, a bit sweet, with a cream cheese filling.

Makes 4 Servings

Cooking + Prep Time: 20 minutes + chilling time

Ingredients:

- 4 crepes, prepared

For filling

- 1 packet of pudding, Jell-o®
- 1 packet of cream cheese, light
- 1 packet of dessert, Danish
- Whipped cream, reduced fat

Instructions:

1. Warm the crepes while you prepare the filling.

2. Make the pudding using the instructions on the box. Combine it with the cream cheese. Combine well and then chill.

3. Make the Danish dessert using package instructions. Chill this, too.

4. Fill crepes with the filling and roll. Top with the Danish style dessert and whipped cream. Serve.

25 – Tiramisu Crepes

These are delicate and intricate crepes, filled with mascarpone cheese, while laced with a bit of coffee flavor liqueur and vanilla. They are a special treat, and quite mouthwatering.

Makes 10 Servings

Cooking + Prep Time: 55 minutes + 1 hour chilling time

Ingredients:

- 4 eggs, large
- 3/4 cup of milk, 2%
- 1/4 cup of club soda, regular
- 3 tbsp. of melted butter, unsalted
- 2 tbsp. of coffee, brewed strong
- 1 tsp. of vanilla extract, pure
- 1 cup of flour, all-purpose
- 3 tbsp. of sugar, granulated
- 2 tbsp. of cocoa, baking
- 1/4 tsp. of salt, kosher

For the filling

- 1 x 8-oz. carton of cheese, mascarpone
- 1 x 8-oz. pkg. of softened cream cheese, low-fat
- 1 cup of sugar, granulated
- 1/4 cup of liqueur, coffee
- 2 tbsp. of vanilla extract, pure

Toppings, optional: additional baking cocoa, chocolate syrup, whipped cream

Instructions:

1. In large mixing bowl, beat milk, club soda, coffee, vanilla, butter and eggs. Combine cocoa, sugar, flour and kosher salt. Add dry mixture to the egg mixture. Combine well. Cover bowl. Place in refrigerator for an hour.

2. Grease a non-stick skillet lightly. Heat on med. Pour 2 tbsp. of batter in middle of the skillet. Swirl pan and evenly coat the bottom thinly. Cook till the top looks dry. Flip. Cook for 12-18 seconds more. Remove to wire rack.

3. Repeat step 2 with the rest of the batter. Grease the skillet when needed.

4. To prepare the filling, beat sugar and cheeses in large mixing bowl till fluffy. Add vanilla and liqueur and beat till smooth. Add 2 tbsp. of filling down middle of crepes and roll them up. Top with your choice of toppings above. Serve.

26 – Ricotta Cinnamon Dessert Crepes

These crepes offer ricotta cheese and cinnamon as a taste treat. The classic flavors of Fall are very much at home in a yummy treat.

Makes 10-15 Servings

Cooking + Prep Time: 15 minutes

Ingredients:

- 12 crepes, prepared
- 1 x 15-oz. container of ricotta cheese, whole milk
- 3 tbsp. of sugar, granulated
- 1 tbsp. of cinnamon, ground

Instructions:

1. Warm the crepes.

2. Mix all filling ingredients together.

3. Spread the mixture on crepes evenly. Serve.

27 – Chocolate, Banana Hazelnut Crepes

This is a delicious yet simple treat. The tender and thin crepes are filled with sautéed bananas and chocolate hazelnut spread, for an elegant look and great taste.

Makes 10 Servings

Cooking + Prep Time: 35 minutes + chilling time

Ingredients:

- 2 eggs, large, whole
- 2 whites from large eggs
- 3/4 cup of water, filtered
- 1/2 cup of milk, 2%
- 1 tbsp. of oil, canola
- 1 cup of flour, all-purpose
- 1 tbsp. of sugar, granulated
- 1/2 tsp. of salt, kosher
- 2 tbsp. of butter, unsalted
- 2 tbsp. of sugar, brown
- 4 peeled, sliced bananas, medium
- 1/3 cup of Nutella® hazelnut chocolate spread

Instructions:

1. In large mixing bowl, whisk together water, oil, milk, eggs and egg whites. Combine sugar, flour and kosher salt. Add dry mixture to egg mixture. Combine well and place in refrigerator for an hour.

2. Grease medium skillet and heat to med. Pour about 1/4 cup of the batter in middle of skillet. Swirl and coat pan evenly and thinly. Cook till top of crepe is dry. Flip. Cook for 13-18 seconds more. Remove crepe to wire rack.

3. Repeat that step with the rest of your batter. Place wax paper between crepes and stack when all are cooked.

4. Melt butter on med-low in skillet. Add and stir in the brown sugar. Blend well. Add the bananas. Cook them for two to three minutes till softened slightly and glazed, while gently stirring them. Remove from heat.

5. Spread the Nutella® on crepes. Top them with the sautéed bananas. Roll and serve.

28 – Banana Cream Dessert Crepes

We made these crepes as a family cooking project and it was their first time using banana cream. It turned out so well that we have these crepes often.

Makes 6 Servings

Cooking + Prep Time: 35 minutes

Ingredients:

- 6 crepes, pre-made
- 3 tbsp. of flour, all-purpose
- 1/3 cup of sugar, granulated
- 4 tsp. of corn starch
- A dash of salt, kosher
- 2 cups of milk, 2%
- 2 yolks from large eggs
- 1 tbsp. of butter, unsalted
- 1 1/2 tsp. of vanilla, pure
- 1 diced large or 2 diced medium bananas

Instructions:

1. Combine the flour, corn starch, sugar and kosher salt in small pan. Add in the milk gradually.

2. Stir while cooking on low heat till mixture thickens.

3. Blend some of this mixture into the egg yolks.

4. Stir the yolks into pan. Cook for a minute. Then remove pan from heat.

5. Add the butter and vanilla and allow to cool.

6. Fold in the diced bananas. Place filling on crepes. Roll them up. Serve.

29 – Cherry Chocolate Crepes

These crepes look impressive when you serve them, but they're simple to make. You can make the crepes and the filling ahead of time, so you'll just assemble and heat them when ready to serve.

Makes 6 Servings

Cooking + Prep Time: 25 minutes

Ingredients:

- 1 x 21-oz. can of pie filling, cherry
- 1 tsp. of almond extract, pure
- 2/3 cup of milk, 2%
- 2 eggs, large
- 2 tbsp. of melted butter, unsalted
- 1/4 cup of ground almonds, blanched
- 1/4 cup of flour, all-purpose

For the filling

- 1 cup of whipping cream, heavy
- 3 oz. of melted, cooled chocolate, semi-sweet
- 1/4 cup of toasted almonds, slivered

Instructions:

1. In small mixing bowl, combine almond extract with cherry pie filling. Cover bowl. Place in the refrigerator to chill.

2. Place milk, butter, eggs, flour and almonds in food processor. Cover. Process till you have a smooth texture.

3. Heat a skillet on med. heat. Add a bit of butter. Pour 2 tbsp. of batter in middle of pan. Swirl pan, coating bottom thinly and evenly. Cook till bottom of crepe is golden brown. Flip and cook for 14-18 more seconds. Remove crepe to plate.

4. Repeat with the rest of the batter. Add butter to skillet when needed. Place sheets of wax paper between crepes and stack till ready for use.

5. In medium bowl, beat the cream with melted chocolate till it forms soft peaks. Spoon 2 tbsp. each on crepes. Top them with the cherry mixture. Sprinkle slivered almonds on top. Serve.

30 – French Crepe Suzettes

These are traditionally fancy, flaming French dessert crepes, but they work well for elegant desserts at home, too. Most of the alcohol will burn off within flames.

Makes 10 Servings

Cooking + Prep Time: 1 hour 5 minutes

Ingredients:

- 6 eggs, large
- 1 cup plus 2 tbsp. of flour, all-purpose
- 1 1/2 tbsp. of sugar, granulated
- 3/4 tsp. of salt, kosher
- 3 cups of milk, low-fat

To fry: butter, unsalted

For the sauce:

- 1 1/2 sticks of butter, unsalted
- 1/3 cup of sugar, granulated
- 3/4 cup of orange juice, fresh if available
- 1/3 cup + 3 tbsp. of liqueur, orange
- 3-4" strip of peel from fresh orange
- 6 tbsp. of cognac

Instructions:

1. Beat eggs, then add the flour, salt and sugar. Beat till you have a smooth texture. Add milk gradually while constantly beating.

2. Melt a tsp. of butter in medium pan. Add 2 tbsp. batter and swirl pan to cover bottom thinly. Cook till bottom of crepe is golden brown. Turn and cook other side till it is light brown in color.

3. Repeat this step till you have used up batter. Transfer crepes to sheets of wax paper as you make them.

4. Melt the butter in a chafing dish. Add the orange juice, orange peel, 1/3 cup of orange liqueur and sugar. Cook till mixture is bubbly and has reduced a bit, five minutes or so. Remove orange peel.

5. Dip the crepes in this heated mixture. Fold them into quarters. Place in pan and push to one side. When you have folded all the crepes, sprinkle with extra sugar and add cognac and last 3 tbsp. of orange liqueur.

6. To ignite the dish, take just one spoonful of the sauce and light it. Quickly pour into the dish. Spoon the sauce over the crepes. Serve.

Conclusion

This French crepes cookbook has shown you…

How to use different ingredients to affect unique tastes in crepes both well-known and rare. You'll learn why crepes are so popular.

How can you include crepes in your home recipe repertoire?

You can…

- Make a golden egg and blueberry breakfast crepes, which you've probably heard of before. They are just as tasty as you have heard.
- Learn to cook with jams, preserves and jellies, which are widely used in making French crepes. Find them in the jam and jelly aisle at your local supermarket.
- Enjoy making delectable seafood crepes, including salmon, crab, and shrimp. Seafood is a mainstay in crepes, and there are SO many ways to make it great.
- Make French crepes using meats and veggies, which are often used in crepes.
- Make various types of desserts like cherry chocolate crepes and French Crepe Suzettes, which will tempt your family's sweet tooth.

Have fun experimenting! Enjoy the results!

About the Author

Allie Allen developed her passion for the culinary arts at the tender age of five when she would help her mother cook for their large family of 8. Even back then, her family knew this would be more than a hobby for the young Allie and when she graduated from high school, she applied to cooking school in London. It had always been a dream of the young chef to study with some of Europe's best and she made it happen by attending the Chef Academy of London.

After graduation, Allie decided to bring her skills back to North America and open up her own restaurant. After 10 successful years as head chef and owner, she decided to sell her business and pursue other career avenues. This monumental decision led Allie to her true calling, teaching. She also started to write e-books for her students to study at home for practice. She is now the proud author of several e-books and gives private and semi-private cooking lessons to a range of students at all levels of experience.

Stay tuned for more from this dynamic chef and teacher when she releases more informative e-books on cooking and baking in the near future. Her work is infused with stores and anecdotes you will love!

Author's Afterthoughts

I can't tell you how grateful I am that you decided to read my book. My most heartfelt thanks that you took time out of your life to choose my work and I hope you find benefit within these pages.

There are so many books available today that offer similar content so that makes it even more humbling that you decided to buying mine.

Tell me what you thought! I am eager to hear your opinion and ideas on what you read as are others who are looking for a good book to buy. Leave a review on Amazon.com so others can benefit from your wisdom!

With much thanks,

Allie Allen

Printed in Great Britain
by Amazon